*piano* ✳ *vocal* ✳ *guitar*

# BEST OF

# WYNONNA

ISBN 0-634-00754-8

**HAL•LEONARD®**
**CORPORATION**

7777 W. BLUEMOUND RD. P.O. BOX 13819 MILWAUKEE, WI 53213

Visit Hal Leonard Online at
**www.halleonard.com**

# BEST OF
# WYNONNA

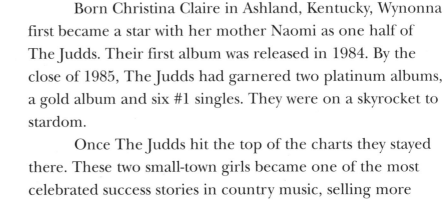

## ✥ BIOGRAPHY ✥

Born Christina Claire in Ashland, Kentucky, Wynonna first became a star with her mother Naomi as one half of The Judds. Their first album was released in 1984. By the close of 1985, The Judds had garnered two platinum albums, a gold album and six #1 singles. They were on a skyrocket to stardom.

Once The Judds hit the top of the charts they stayed there. These two small-town girls became one of the most celebrated success stories in country music, selling more than twenty million records and winning over sixty industry awards including five Grammies, nine Country Music Association awards and eight Billboard Music awards.

Throughout the '80s it looked as if there was no end to success for this dynamic duo. But in October of 1990, Naomi learned she had contracted Hepatitis C. After a lifetime of dreams and six years at the top, Naomi had to retire. On December 4, 1991, The Judds performed their final concert. It was the end of an era.

Wynonna released her first solo album in 1992. With critical acclaim, it became the highest-selling debut record by a female artist. (The record was later broken by LeAnn Rimes.) A year later *Tell Me Why* gained platinum status and was followed by the introspective *revelations* (1996), her final Curb/MCA album *Collection* (1997) and *The Other Side* (1997).

As a solo artist, Wynonna has sold more than nine million records and celebrated thirteen top ten hits. Adored by fans and admired by peers, she has become a superstar in her own right.

WYNONNA

## ✥ WYNONNA... ✥

**On the music business:** "After fifteen years in the music business I don't feel like I have to prove anything. Between 18 and 30, I spent a lot of time trying to be everything everyone wanted me to be. It's so funny to be a veteran artist at 34 but I can really feel the strength of what I've learned and what I know. Now I just try to do my own thing, hoe my own row. It's really incredible. I can just follow my heart. And it's not about arrogance. It's about confidence."

**On her upcoming album:** "As I begin the process of a new record, I feel the spark and the energy of a new beginning. I'm in a place in my life where I'm so grateful to be in country music and to sing the music I love. Let's face it: this is a competitive industry. But for me it's not about trying to pave the new road to success. All I want to do is make a connection. And I do that through music. That is my gift. If I stay true to myself and true to the music, if I strive for excellence in singing music that I love, then what is meant to be will be. That sounds so simple, but it has taken me so long to understand the concept."

**On songs:** "Finding the right songs is like walking into a room and there are, say, a hundred people there. But you're drawn to just two or three of them—one inspires you, another reminds you of someone you love. You're drawn to the ones that tug at your heart."

**On reuniting with her mother Naomi for a New Year's Eve 1999 concert:** "Since 1991, Mom and I have sung together at church and with my kids. That's it. Singing with her again causes me to still feel the joy and pain of our history together. The past reminds me of the loss and having to accept God's new plan for my life in 1992. The present is bringing me great joy. The present is definitely a 'present,' a gift."

## ❖ ABOUT WYNONNA... ❖

*Newsweek*: "Wynonna can sing like a dream. She's got the most exhilarating voice in country today—not just pretty, but full of depth and dimension, with a sweet, whispery top and a bluesy bottom growl."

*The Los Angeles Times*: "Wynonna may just be the most complete and gifted female singer of her generation—and we're not just talking country music."

*Billboard*: "Wynonna explores a song's every emotional nuance. Without a trace of grandstanding or vocal theatrics that a lesser artist might employ, she can wrap a lyric around her heart and sing like a woman who has lived every line."

*The New York Daily News*: "Wynonna attacks tunes with ferocious passion."

*Houston Chronicle*: "Her stylistic choices breathe life into the increasingly stale world of female country singers. Coupled with her talent is Wynonna's saucy sense of style...she practically oozes hipness."

*Orange County Register*: "Wynonna keeps turning out gem after gem. She's still the one to beat. Hands down."

*Hollywood Reporter*: "Wynonna expresses the joys and agonies of romantic love in the most emotionally direct terms imaginable. Her vocals demonstrate a singular talent and her ingratiating personality is undeniably infectious."

*Dallas Morning News*: "Wynonna is a force of nature with her volcanic hair and majestic voice."

# COME SOME RAINY DAY

Words and Music by BILLY KIRSCH
and BAT McGRATH

*Original Key: G♭ major. This edition has been transposed up one half-step to be more playable.*

# HEAVEN HELP MY HEART

Words and Music by DAVID TYSON,
TINA ARENA and DEAN McTAGGART

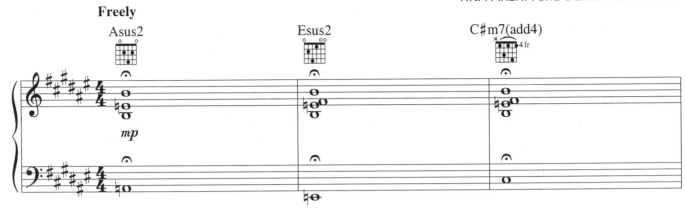

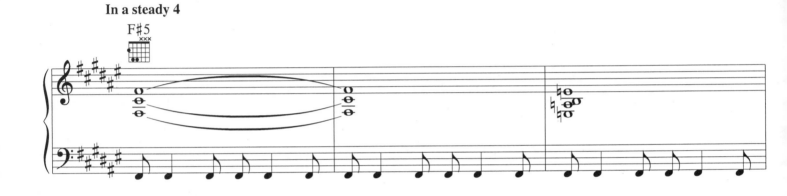

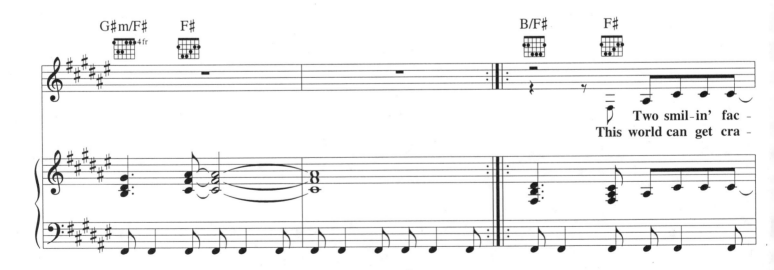

Two smil-in' fac -
This world can get cra -

Heav-en help _ my heart _

# I SAW THE LIGHT

Words and Music by LISA ANGELLE
and ANDREW GOLD

22

23

# IS IT OVER YET

Words and Music by
BILLY KIRSCH

**Slow ballad**

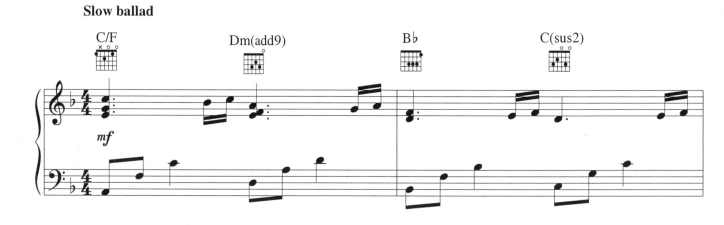

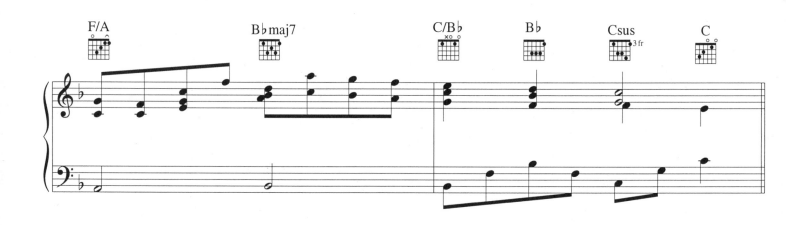

Tell    me when          I can o - pen my    eyes. ___
The tax - i's wait  –  ing     in the drive - way for    you. ___

# MY STRONGEST WEAKNESS

Words and Music by NAOMI JUDD
and MIKE REID

# NO ONE ELSE ON EARTH

Words and Music by SAM LORBER,
STEWART HARRIS and JILL COLUCCI

# ONLY LOVE

Words and Music by MARCUS HUMMON
and ROGER MURRAH

I have
sailed a boat _ or two, out on the wild _ blue _ yon-
wa-ters, rag-in' sea, it is all the same _ to me. I can
der to dreams _ that rare-ly come true. _
close my eyes _____ and still be free. _

# ROCK BOTTOM

Words and Music by BUDDY BUIE
and J.R. COBB

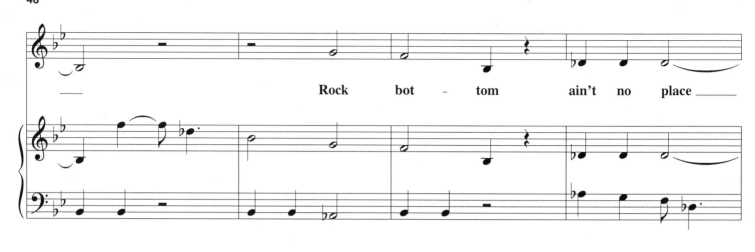

Rock bot - tom ain't no place ___

**To Coda**

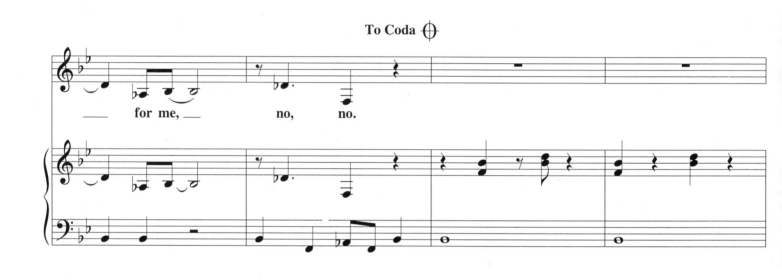

for me, ___ no, no.

No, ___ no. ___

# SHE IS HIS ONLY NEED

Words and Music by
DAVE LOGGINS

# TO BE LOVED BY YOU

Words and Music by GARY BURR
and MIKE REID

# TELL ME WHY

Words and Music by
KARLA BONOFF

# WHEN LOVE STARTS TALKIN'

Words and Music by JAMIE O'HARA,
BRENT MAHER and GARY NICHOLSON

When love starts talk-in', you got no choice but to shut up and lis-ten— it's a pow-er-ful voice.

**Repeat and Fade**

When